DAZZLING LIFE

AN ANTHOLOGY OF POEMS

VARIOUS

ISBN 979-888521116-1

To people and Life

Contents

Dr. Rosie Patangia

1. My First Love 3
2. Between The Stars 4
3. My Daughters 5
4. Seven Days Of The Week In A Foreign Land 6
5. A Trip To Darjeeling 8
6. My Dearest Friend 10
7. A Haunted House 11
8. The Bamboos 12
9. Sir Isaac Newton 13
10. Teacher 14

Tanya Goyel

11. Nation's Journey 17
12. Bestfriend 18
13. Hope 20
14. Listening To Music 21
15. There Was A Man Of Sicily 23

Ritu Kumari

16. First Love 27
17. Between Stars 28
18. Point Of View Of One Of My Parents 29
19. पहला गीत 30
20. Hope 31
21. Meaning Of Life 32

Contents

22. Communication With Trees	33
23. I'm God	34
24. I'm Alexander Bell	35
Mitali Vinod Rathod	
25. First	39
26. A Magical Night	40
27. Demons Of The Night	42
28. The Sky Is Pink	44
29. This Too Shall Pass	45
30. I Miss You	46
31. Flames	48
32. The Source Of Our Life	49
33. The Apple Man	51
34. My Moon	52
Farah Naseem	
35. Light And Shadow	57
36. First Time Meeting An Ocean	58
37. My Son	60
38. Peregrinate Tenor	61
39. Monotony Of Life	63
40. Gist, A Seed In The Garden	64
41. Zehava Incarcerate	65
42. Temptation	68
43. Trouvaille Rondure	69

Contents

44. Vernal Equinox 70

Jasmine Panda

45. Love At First Sight 73

46. Dream, Dream And Dream 75

47. आइना 76

48. Never-ending Footsteps 78

49. The Beginning 79

50. Remember! 82

51. Magic Of The Majesty 83

52. Celebration Of Womanhood 85

Ramandeep Kaur

53. जज्बात 91

54. अंजान सपने 92

55. माँ 93

56. दोस्ती 94

57. आशा 95

58. जिंदगी 96

59. बंद राजकुमारी 98

60. विश्वास 99

61. भगवान हूं 100

Bikash Singh

62. बेटी 105

63. आज के युवा 107

Contents

64. दहेज प्रथा 109

65. सजा 111

66. बचपन 112

67. बछिर गये 114

68. कहानी 115

Rohit Gupta

69. पहली बार खुद को नराश कयिा 119

70. मखौटे के पीछे 120

71. एक बहुत बढ़ा व्यक्त 121

72. अवकाश स्मृत 122

73. ईश्वर पूरी कर दे मुराद मेरी 123

Dr. Rosie Patangia

Dr. Rosie Patangia is an Assistant Professor and Head in the Department of English, Narangi Anchalik Mahavidyalaya, Guwahati, Assam, India. She has done her Ph.D. from the Department of Folklore Research, Gauhati University. She is a bilingual poet and has co-authored various poetry Anthologies, and many are on the way. Her poems have been published in various newspapers and magazines and translated into Tamil, Telugu, and Gujarati. She has a number of publications in books, research journals, peer-reviewed journals, edited volumes on literature and Folklore. She has presented papers in National and International Seminars and Conferences and has received best paper awards for her research papers on folklore. Furthermore, she has also received the Certificate of Appreciation, Teacher Innovation Award from Sri Aurobindo Society (ZIIEI) in 2019 for Sustainable Efforts towards promoting joyful and Experiential teaching. She is a lifelong member of All India Association for Educational Research, the Indian National Trust for Art and Cultural Heritage, and Assam Sahitya Sabha. Besides, she loves traveling and painting.

Instagram ID: @dr.rosiepatangia

1. My First Love

You are my first love
You came like a white dove
You sat beside me
My soul became free.
I felt an ecstatic joy
And was a bit coy
You touched my hands
And wrote my name in the rocks and sand.
I felt in my body a sudden shiver
Like a flowing river
You expressed your profound love
And tried to prove.
I saw your face glow
As you sat inside the bungalow
You kissed my forehead
And expressed your warmth.
Soon we had to depart
Only to reunite
After a fortnight
It was already past midnight

2. Between The Stars

On this cold October night
I can see you look so bright
You sparkle, you glitter
You are my shining star.
As I fly towards you
Like a bird in the sky
My wings spread
And becomes fluffy and red.
You keep shining day and night.
But you are visible only at night
I shout, I scream.
I want you to fulfill my dream.
I love you like the way you are
But you are so far
Still, you are my shining star.
And also my superstar.

3. My Daughters

My daughters are the epitome of beauty
They are so sincere in their duty
They love to watch the television
At times, they help me in the kitchen.
When they are happy, they jump and run
They express their merriment and fun
They love to play word puzzles or sing when they are free
They are like tiny birds sitting on a tree.
At times, they both fight
For a pen or shirt
They are, no doubt, brilliant
They always look fresh and radiant.

I always marvel
To see their joy when they travel
They love to eat an apple
Or a pineapple.
May God shower them with all joy
As they go out and enjoy.

4. Seven Days of The Week in a Foreign Land

On a Monday morning, my brother and I boarded our flight
to Iran
Our minds were filled with great excitement and fun.
Inside the flight, we were served hot coffee
We felt so relaxed and free.
On Tuesday we reached the airport, and it was already night
And everything looked so peaceful and quiet.
We took a car and reached the city
Our hearts were beating fast with curiosity.
With the advent of Wednesday, we passed through the Tabiat
Pedestrian bridge
Ah! Its dazzling design made me freeze
It was studded with pink light
And was a majestic sight.
Thursday arrived and we booked a night bus to Isfahan
And was mesmerized by the sight of a sea-fish aquarium and
an amazing museum.
We saw a Zoroastrian temple on top of a hill
We found a market surrounded by a field.
As Friday came by, we made our way to Persepolis
And was elated to see a hundred pillars that remained as it is.

The Xerxes' gateway, the tall columns, the inscriptions and carvings on the walls and stone
I felt like a king or queen sitting on a throne.
On Saturday we visited the tomb of Khwajeh Shams-al-Din Muhammad Hafez-e- Shirazi
The master of Persian lyric poetry
We also paid homage at the tomb of Sa'di
A place of pilgrimage for the lovers of Persian poetry.
In the afternoon, we saw a woman covering her head with a scarf
And walking over the green turf
She wore a black dress with long sleeves
And looked elegant and unique.
On Sunday we boarded our plane
And on our return, every thing looked well and fine
I sat near the window and watched the clouds that looked lily-white
And the sun shone so bright.
Our journey was now complete
And my dream to see a foreign land was thus accomplished.

5. A Trip to Darjeeling

As part of our college excursion
We went to Darjeeling
With a mind bright
And a soul light.
Nature fascinated us
With all its beauty and might
The sunrise at Tiger Hills
Gave us so much excitement and thrill.
A part of the mountain ranges of the Himalayas
Is the Kanchenjunga
It gave us peaceful vibrations
And wonderful sensations.
The colossal Tensing rock
Our students did climb with their boots and sock
As we set foot on the rock garden carrying out sweater and shawl
We enjoyed the cascading waterfalls.
Atop the hills, the tea-gardens
Looked so fresh, so neat and clean
The Batasia loop, the toy train
We put on the Gurkha traditional dress and ourselves did entertain.
In the Darjeeling zoo

We saw the red Panda too
The trip was so mesmerizing
We shall cherish in our hearts the days we spent in Darjeeling.

6. My Dearest Friend

You are my dearest friend
You stay beside me in my dire need
At times, you inspire me
You are like a bird, so carefree.
You express your profound care
A friend like you is precious and rare.
You show your pure and unconditional love
Like a star from above.
The moment I recall our childhood days
That was so golden like the sun's rays
The days we spent in school
Were the best days of our life and so cool.
Dear friend, now you live in my mind, my memory
You linger in my soul as you are so extraordinary
When I remember you
I feel so happy, like the morning dew.

7. A Haunted House

Walking through a forest once
I came across a haunted house
The path looked dreary
It was so strange and fiery.
Soon I heard a noise
I was so alarmed and forgot my poise
A spirit seemed to surround the haunted house
All thoughts of fear in me arouse.
Soon, evening set in
I was wondering how to return from within
It was a thick jungle
And I began to fumble.
So bizarre the surrounding
No movement of humans encircling
At last I reached home safe and sound
And sat in the playground.
And rejoiced to my heart's content
Feeling grateful and potent.

8. The Bamboos

The Bamboos as a part of Nature
The bamboos lower their heads and create shadows
As the wind blows in the meadow
They show their humility and respect
For all the creatures on this earth and beyond.
These bamboos beat the rain
Sometimes I observe them from my garden
They seem to look towards heaven
To receive God's grace and blessings.
The bamboos know the storm won't last forever
The sun will again shine over and over
Then these bamboos will again dance
In the light of the morning sun, I surmise.

9. Sir Isaac Newton

Sir Isaac Newton, was a great mathematician and scientist
He was truly very intelligent
Unlocking all his burden
One day he sat in his garden.
Suddenly he saw an apple falling from a tree
He remained silent but was not satisfied to any degree
He was wondering why the apple fell from the tree
And tried to find out with his reason of his curiosity.
He kept thinking why the apple fell from the tree
Just near his seat and knee
He decided to find out the cause
This led him to formulate the laws of motion and gravitation

10. Teacher

Who is a teacher?
Isn't he a giver?
Of knowledge, of wisdom
And make his students free from boredom.
The teacher teaches
At times, he preaches
He teaches with full devotion
And tries to catch the student's attention.
The teacher stands for values and wisdom
He expresses his views with full freedom
He motivates and inspires his students
And shapes their future generations.
We should respect our teacher
As he is our well-wisher
He guides us and shows the light
And makes our life bright.

Tanya Goyel

Tanya Goyel is in standard 12th pursuing commerce stream. She loves to ink with words. She writes poems, quotes, and short stories. Not only that, but she is part of many anthologies too. She is an avid learner and an explorer. She believes is Karma rather than just yelling.

Here is her write-up. Hope you all love her poetry while going through it.

11. Nation's Journey

A journey from the agony of partition to a strong, powerful, and developing nation.
Leaving behind a string of each and every landmark.
A Journey from being torn down by Britishers,
The designing and making Asia's 1st nuclear reactor.
A Journey from begging for food from Americans,
The launching of the Green Revolution initiative, increasing production,
A Journey from lacking in technologies,
To designing India's 1st Space Satellite in 1975.
A Journey from spotting the match from the exterior,
To winning 1st Cricket World Cup by defeating West Indies.
A Journey from ruining owns state and provinces,
To successfully recapturing Tiger Hill in the War Of Kargil.
A Journey from starting of black marketing,
To Demonetization and making GST effective.
It's a very vast Journey,
From life's expedition to having Universe.

12. Bestfriend

What to say, about a friend like you
Is hard to find…
I make fun of you each and every time.
I know your weaknesses,
And you know my strength…
That's the reason of our strong bond, and that's great.
Friendship with you is mine asset…
And a small fight with you is decrease in it...
I don't believe in giving friendship bracelets…
But in sharing my deep thoughts, and that's my concern.
Sharing with you lots of happy times…
Too sharing, sometimes tears…
And you are my partner in every crime…
Not going to leave you anyhow, I swear.
Whenever I talk to you,
I just forget my worries…
Without you, I am like…
Life without oxygen, living obsolescence.
From life hardships to life's happiness…
From heartbreak to soulmates…
You always stood there, and that's your goodness.
And I'll always be there for you to frustrate.
Starting from childhood…

Ending when the dust bites me…
This long-lasting friendship…
Is made with tolerance and patience.
With you, I have bundles of eidetic.
And your presence to me is an addiction…
Like drugs to a drug addict…
And in your absence, sadness is conspicuous.
Our friendship is not limited…
Within the boundaries of caste and creed…
Whether it is worth it or not,
I'm going to rely on your each and every deed.
The longevity of our friendship…
Is not bound of good days…
With you, I have feelings of belonging,
I know, you are my gift of amazed.
You explained to me the true value of life…
A friend like you cannot be undermined…
Thank you for your healthy advice…
Making fun of you is responsibility, don't ever mind…!!

13. Hope

Let's have a visit in the World Of Joy,
Everything being so perfect on the utopia globe.
Flawlessly, people giving their own exertion and toil,
No jealousy with each other on this soil.
No Green Wars, and wars of gas and fire,
People roaming all around with brothers, forbidding, conspire.
The world which gives view of paradise,
No mind gamed and everyone is live and no inflation in price.
Absence of poverty and discriminatory challenges,
No case of suicide and truant terror and unkindness.
The mart of power, the fount of will,
The source and bound of good and ill will be every evil.
Free-minded from tensions and stress,
Everyone, from continuous work, will take some rest.
Sharing love and concern with each and every country,
Living there, all'll be free,
If we truly wish to be.

14. Listening to music

Listening to music,
More than listening to people,
Maybe I could be
misunderstood by public,
But music feel me,
I feel music,
Acknowledges and makes me
feel soothing.
You are my favorite song
Of mine,
Which I keep on playing.
It rehabilitates my soul.
Its always
on the repeat mode,
Is the song
which shows the reality of every moon.
This gives me sympathy and courage too.
The song Memories by Maroon5
Reflects the human's actuality of Life.
It taught me to enjoy
The moment I have,
Rather than hoping for more good and reminiscing the past.
As we don't know about pain in our childhood,

But now no one last forever,
Sign of adulthood.
Impact of this song
on my mundane
Is like oxygen for life.
Is like water for aquatic animals.
I can listen to it
All night- day long
Whether I am sad,
Or in a mood of delirium.
In this song,
Nothing could be wrong.
For me, this song is like,
Open door to my soul.

15. There was a man of Sicily

There was a man of Sicily, named Archimedes
Who pursued a life of thought and invention.
A workaholic person of wisdom,
Saying "Give me a lever and a place to stand, and I'll move the world".
A person who was so focused on solving a mathematical problem,
Ordered by Marcellus, to be buried with honors.
One day, in his experimental period, charged himself,
Proving that the Hieron king's crown was not pure gold.
A day, he filled a bathtub and noticed,
Water spilled over the edge as he got in and realized.
The weight of the body was as the same,
As the water displaced by his body.
Helped to know that gold was heavier from other metals,
In which the crown maker have substituted.
He went running down the streets shouting_ 'Eureka',
Forgetting, he was undressed and naked.
And from then onwards, a Principle was made, which stated-
"buoyant force on an object submerged in a fluid is equal to the weight of the fluid that is displaced by that object."

And finally the day arrived, he discovered the principle of buoyancy,
Which marked it as the best-known achievement - Eureka Moment.

Ritu Kumari

Ritu Kumari was born on 15 May 1995 I live in New Delhi. I am

Hard-working

Determinant

Obstinate

Optimistic

Confide

16. First love

Love is always special.
It is a wonderful feeling
For me, first love was never some
Another person, always it was me...
Without knowing yourself, how someone can fall for some other person???
Love is within you...
Your first love is only you
First fall in love with yourself
Love means nothing but you
It starts from you, then you spread it
all over the world...
Love means you ..
Love yourself first...

17. Between Stars

It was dark night
A frightened girl was standing alone at a site
Then, suddenly, She saw something bright in the alone night
the light was coming from a star
Now, all her fear gone so far
Wearing a smile on her face,
She moved with the pace
Far from the all rat race
Now, in between the stars, she is the
Happiest soul, As she knows she is very close to her goal.

18. Point of view of one of my parents

One day you will realize all that rebuke to you was just to teach you some lessons
A lesson that will make you a better person
A version of your past,
A healthy mind, people who motivate others to do so
As a child you gave us smile and all happen, so as a parent it's my onus to make your life and future blessed,
Became a person who works for humanity.
You spread smile and happiness in your childhood, So the same you do in your adulthood...

19. पहला गीत

उनका वो भेजा पहला गीत आज भी याद हैं हमें,
संगीत के माध्यम से उनका मेरी यादों आ जाना
आज भी याद हैं हमें
गीतों के वो अल्फ़ाज़ सुनकर कैसे मुस्कुरा देते थे वो,
उनका वो मुस्कुराना आज भी याद हमें
फिर एक दिन उनका मुझसे मुंह मोड़कर चले जाना,
आज भी याद हैं हमें
उनका वो भेजा हुआ पहला संगीत आज भी याद हैं हमें

20. Hope

Life goes on expectations and hope,
Keep up the good work and move happily in your journey
Sometimes life will feel worthy,
Sometimes not
But we all are alive in the hope of good thing
You have to rely on the ray of hope,
As we all experienced, we all have to suffer at different phases of life
What keeps you moving on??
It is the only hope which makes you move forward in your journey.
Always work for the best and hope for the best..

21. Meaning of Life

Hey listen, Life is really blessed when you see it from an optimistic perspective.

Yeah, I agree it has pain and sufferings too, but that comes across your way to teach you a lesson.

A lesson that will make you wiser and stronger, and a better version of yourself than before.

Don't get disappointed as this will only bless you with a New You.

Life is blessed if you see it from my point of view

Live, love your life and make it even more Beautiful..

22. Communication with Trees

Hey, I saw you are always standing at one place, don't you get bored ?? (I asked)

No, because I can see Greenery around myself. (tree replied)

But don't you have any work to do ??? (I Asked)

The tree replied: don't you know? You are standing in front of me because I gave you oxygen in the air in which you can breathe easily, I gave you food to eat, you eat different fruits because of me, when it's cold it's my branches that you burn to keep yourself warm. Now, say am, I don't do any work for you???

I said: No, you have made my life easier than I think Hmm, that's really kind of you, and I'm really grateful to you...

Tree said: but I don't know why people still cut me down for their own benefits

I said: Now, this time, I'll do something for you.

What will you do?? (Tree asked)

I'll tell people the importance of you.

I'll tell you are very important for us to survive, without you our life will be hell

You are equally important as any other human being.

Tree: that's really sweet of you..

23. I'm God

There are so many sufferings and pain in the world, as we have witnessed several deaths around us in this pandemic.

People were so helpless, small children were losing their only parent... There was so much hustle in recent days

If I'm God, first

I'll remove the suffering from the life of children who lost their parents in this pandemic, as they are the most innocent creatures on this planet earth. They did nothing wrong but are still in pain.

Second.

I'll help the children who are living in extreme conditions, as these children also deserve some betterment in their lives

I'll make available houses for them, food to eat and proper clothes to wear.

Third

I'll keep no child as an orphan because all the children deserve the love of their parents.

Fourth

I'll make sure the children who left their parents in their old age are punished at any cost. As they deserve the lesson.

24. I'm Alexander Bell

Do you miss your grandparents??

Do you want to talk to them??

You don't need to miss them

I have invented a special gadget through which you can easily talk to your grandparents.

You can use the telephone at any time and at any place.

Now, distance is not a matter for all of us

It will create no barrier in your communication with anyone.

It is not very expensive, and it is really quick and easy to use.

You can talk about confidential matters as well

As other people can't hear your communication.

Mitali Vinod Rathod

Hi, you lovely people! My name is Mitali, and I also go by ***myth***, my pen name. My pronouns are She/her. I'm an old soul filled with melancholy, with the desire to do it all. I'm a selenophile, a lover of the moon, stars, night, and all things alike. Not only that, but I'm also a Dancer for the Heart, a Writer for the Soul, Devil for the mind and a Fighter for the body! That says it all! Loads of Love!

25. First

First touch, first kiss,
first ever feel of true bliss.
First fight, first tear,
first sense of real fear.
Each first was true,
each first were you.
You and me,
we'll make it through.
Each day, each night,
we'll push away the fright.
First promise,
last vow,
I have,
still do,
and will always,
Love thou!

26. A Magical Night

I lay on this earth,
wide awake this night,
under an array of
dazzling stars and the moon,
Breathtaking is the night sky,
the sight, a vision to enthrall
the heart of even a fool.
I'm captivated by the
the beauty of the divine moon,
as all its precious jewels
twinkle and blush and swoon.
I'm enticed by those stars,
those glistening little pearls,
as they form pretty constellations
and twinkle and twirl.
This vision before my eyes
is a magical prize,
for the belief I have
on my moon and the skies.
Just then a few sparks fly
and soar up high into the sky,
and I see the most surreal vision
unravel in front of my eyes.

I see beautiful shooting stars,
not one but, oh my, two,
together they move,
flashing across the night sky,
leaving behind an amorphous dust
and a vibrant little hue.
I've never seen a vision so pure,
ever in my life,
and it gives me new hope to
rise and to live, not just survive.
I see as the stars move across the sky,
together, as if hand in hand,
a sight to soothe the eyes.
They move with a magical force,
a magnificent power to behold,
they destroy everything in their way and
with their immense love, magic unfolds.
Sparks fly and glitters dance,
oh! It is a whirlwind romance.
The night sky is now a magical canvas,
the stars paint with magic and fill this abyss,
with warmth and care and love and light,
they make this night and the world shine bright.

27. Demons of The Night

This night is different,
and yet the same,
once again I feel the weight
of the never-ending pain,
once again I'll be on the
receiving end of the rain,
only this rain is not divine,
not heaven-sent, not sweet,
it is the rain of teardrops
that fall out of precious eyes
and my surface they meet.
I am the pillow that
cries each night,
along with my master,
who holds onto me tight,
as if his next breath
depends upon me,
and if he lets go, he'll fall free.
And so he holds me,
and cries and screams,
it is haunting as if his
monsters are out of his dreams
He fights this long battle each night,

it is strenuous and takes all his might.
But he doesn't let go,
he fights back and looks for the light
the monsters try to break him,
but in the end, give up
In front of his strong fight.
He calms down and his tears fade,
and on by his head he's now laid,
he shivers involuntarily with the fear,
as from his eye slips one line tear,
that tear finally soothes his soul,
as he falls into a deep slumber,
and his demons fall into a black hole

28. The Sky is Pink

Oh dear,
mine love for thee,
is this shade of pink.
The pink I turn,
when thou touch me,
when thou softly caress
every inch of my skin,
oh, how lovely it feels,
it must be a sin.
The pink the sky is this day,
like no other, no way.
A soft blush spread across the sky,
Oh love, isn't it beautiful,
the sky, thou and I?

29. This Too Shall Pass

Hear me, my dear friend, Have faith and Believe,
This too shall pass, and A Euphoric sigh of relief We all shall heave!
Times have changed, life is different, people insane,
the truth of the situation has made them inhumane
Survival is difficult, not impossible yet quite close to it,
Not because of the diseases, but the greedy men's profit.
But not all men are alike, some are wonderful, angels indeed
Come to help all at any point of time with concern for all's needs
Times are tough and the pain ever-increasing,
Old memories bring tears upon reminiscing.
But don't stop, don't quit keep on the fight
We will push away the darkness and bring back the light.
Hear me, my dear friend, Have faith and Believe,
This too shall pass, and A Euphoric sigh of relief We all shall heave!

30. I Miss You

I look up into the sky,
And thy face I see,
All I wish is to fly,
So with thee, I can be.
In every passing moment of grace
I miss thy affectioned face
The face that led me to abeyance
And disrupted normalcy with its mere presence
In every passing moment of despair
I cry 'til my lungs are out of air
With the wish to be united with thee
So under thy protection I can be
In every passing moment of longing
The pain increases in my heart throbbing
It kills me with every beat of my heart
And rips my heart from my body apart
In every passing moment of hope
The longing for you is hard to cope
It burns my heart from the inside out
And increases the agony with each anguished shout
In every passing moment of delight
I fill your absence with soothing light
The light which warms the soul burning bright

Only to remind me of your absence in sight
I miss you with every passing moment
Your absence marks me with a longing
Leaving me with a void so prominent
Which leads me to the brink of belonging
The brink that then fades away
Bringing the pain and the skies gray
That lead me to a demented disarray
Only to bring me to a heartsick dismay.

31. Flames

Burning within
Set fire to the skin
Wild embers akin
To love, 'tis a sin
But I the Devil befriend
Walk the edge of a scend
Leisurely pace the wend
Greet warmly my end
I burn with sparks of desire
Lay bare on the heavenly pyre
Aware of each sense going higher
As flames of ecstasy within transpire

32. The Source of Our Life

The little drops of water,
Tiny grains of sand,
Little buds of flowers,
Tiny little hands.
All so delicate and docile,
Swaying to the rhythm of the wind,
Look so beautiful and fragile,
All under the protection of a heavenly shield.
The shield of mother nature,
woven with love and care,
She looks after each of her children,
protects them everywhere.
She meets all our needs,
provides us with every little thing,
She is the source of our existence
and all our little inklings.
She is our sacred grounds,
heavenly skies and still waters,
She is the sacrifice made to
protect each of earth's daughter.
We stand at the altar of her embrace,
enthralled by her enchanting grace,
She is the embodiment of love and care,

she is our mother, an angelic face.
We are birthed from her eternal roots,
she feeds us all her heavenly fruits.
We are healed by her mystic essence,
she nurtures us with just her presence.
She is the source of our life and all things material,
She is our mother, and her love for us ethereal.

33. The Apple Man

Sitting under a tree, in its cool and calm shade,
I see a man at a distance, under another tree, laid
he was enjoying the bright day in its serene silence,
captivated by his surroundings and their resilience.
Just then, a fruit from the tree falls on his head,
and suddenly he's all up and tensed as if to defend
himself from a ghost that would eat him alive,
and he's got to save himself and fight to survive.
But he looks at the fruit, an apple indeed, and laughs
and eats it after breaking it into two halves.
I sit and laugh to myself, thinking what a fool,
got scared by an apple and nearly lost his cool.
The man, then I see, is now deep in thought,
worried about something, his face distraught.
He seems to be thinking about something very important
because he looks back and forth between
the ground and the tree, as if all this while he's been ignorant.
Out of nowhere, he gets up and runs somewhere,
as if he found the cure to stop the greying of hair.
But he runs out of the garden like his life depends upon it,
and on his face, there is an expression which says
He found his try calling and all reasons behind it.

34. My Moon

The stars twinkling in your presence
driven to you by your charismatic
essence; captivated in the void
by your divine fragrance
bound to you
by a promise
of an exquisite
ecstatic
romance
I envy those stars, their close presence
to you, them having a feel of your
sweet essence; of being able to
inhale your celestial fragrance
I wish to be the one instead
bound to you even if
it be only for a
timed
dalliance
you share your light, your warmth
your love with each star everyday
while I long for you so much
from so far away
I cry each night

on bed as I lay
to be one
with you
someday
and fall asleep
chanting your name
as the tears on
my cheeks
fade
away

Farah Naseem

Farah Naseem born in Bhopal, as childhood includes all creative tasks, had motivated me towards writing. After appreciation from parents started writing on Blog, Facebook, Instagram, and YourQuote.

Worked as lecturer Microbiologist in Medical College and Pharma companies, right now working as Deputy Manager in Chennai. But my enthusiasm for writing always remains high. Participated in few anthologies. My hobbies include writing short stories and essay writing and some spicy fantasy as well as friction.

35. Light and Shadow

Caught in between light and shadow,
Like water Mellon with black seeds and sand dunes of Colorado,
Running towards dream and nothing can be seized,
Only foot get pain and years with grey rain,
Mid of desire and nothing to be achieved,
Like red apple but raw taste,
Future spark a valley of triumph,
Shadow behind remind one how
to overcome flaws,
Like Moon look at Sun to glow beautiful and bright,
With no own light, a colossus
dumb but still shine at dark night

36. First time meeting an ocean

A house near the seashore,
One can hear the sea waves sound
From very far,
When tides play with the shore, they crumble and reach the window,
White cloudy bubbly salty water,
Evening dark and scary till eyesight reach its black,
But above all, beachcomber shine and enjoy till last,
It's all my imagination before meeting
sea surge,
While going near the sea, its different emotions and feelings,
When waves touch my feet, it's amazing and weird,
Prodigious notion and splendor thought,
Scintillating fervor was about to whim,
Impetus turns all colorful, its magic of
beach full of spiffy,
Life is not much different from the beach,
A small tide is just similar to a kid,
With time, it learns and grows,
Then turn into a beautiful adult who knows how to restraint and aplomb,
Next is nothing but knock off and abate,

It's all life draw out from nothing to best.

37. My Son

As a mom, while holding ink to write about him,
Mostly just lost all the feelings thread,
All phrases will lose their soul, he is so calm and cool,
Colossal is not his part, rather he is mammoth with spark,
He is like a drop of water so pure, settle on leaf with Vibgyor,
He is a flower who will spread fragrance so vast,
An asunder and blithe, so rutilant,
Virescent, and appears as Zephyr,
Beautiful soul from welkin vestal and lucent,
Lay of peace, comely and lilt,
Teach the world rules of halcyon and eloquence.

38. Peregrinate Tenor

It's spring zephyr with golden leaves,
Sun and sky grin in a frolicking way,
Flowers by road pink and yellow,
Teaches one to forget the dolor,
Bicycle with two tires and one seat,
Shoes are ready to beat the self-limit,
Nature let you realize blissful thought,
Some mountains are historic art,
Clouds forming different curves,
Some are faces, some are aught,
A long road with no sign of humans,
Side by are grasses with weed origin,
Bag at back little tilt and shake,
Its camera want to capture Coulisse,
Just a few snaps, some black and white,
Some colored awesome Vista trap,
With passing time again on track,
My goal calling me to join the camp,
From Calicut to Waynad tiring trip,
Zigzag road and mountain twist,
Coconut water pour the thirst,
Deluge footprint one can easily observe,
Houses at some distance now and then,

Root having a print of water stains,
Walls are almost changed in color,
Somewhere it appears as a butterfly,
At some places, it's a black bear,
It's almost four-month from now,
Condition is not changing for now,
As the heaven on earth destination reached,
It's a lovely view with a beautiful fountain,
All-natural, the water and view,
Motorboats running and wooden too,
Garden turn pale with petals of daffodils,
Tea taste awesome after so tiring trip,
Toast with birds chirping taste so crisp,
Waterfall in between the shades,
Let me remember my old days,
Turning the cycle back to Aunty Annie home,
Will surely patch up with memories twist,
Sum up with camp seniors and friends,
Together with uncle aunty and cousin band,
Will help the needy and poor refugees.

39. Monotony of life

Fear of life is not quietus, but it's still one didn't played better,
An annihilation is truth forever,
Every start has an end may be far better,
A bud to flower then cessation veil it,
Birth carry with it doom,
A valley full of tree get damaged by flood,
Water is not life always, sometimes it's dreaded too,
One "on the hoof" and vibrant, but ravage never left one alone,
A nonchalance state will drive one towards nonsense,
Melancholy at old age is nothing, just a state of cachexy,
When worriment are around ones, they live to fight,
But when ennui yashmak only pessimism upset,
It's despondency which play an effective role,
When dysthymia impart gray shade on life rainbow,
Then dénouement and epilog left to play

40. Gist, a seed in the garden

Some brushstrokes little pencil shade,
Shifting clouds and imagination with landscape,
Smell of clay, a way of connecting nature on its bay,
A universal realm and a spatula of hope,
Melody which imprint every emotion imbue,
Beyond once vainglory and thoughts,
Like chimera in desert it fulfill all thirst,
Only artist know how to decorate canvas with specs,
Some splatter to merge all fervour,
Let maggot fly as desore get shaped,
As volition and intent are ones own thoughts,
But to potrate it in best way is called craft.

41. Zehava incarcerate

Beautiful eyes and long hairs,
She is so different and cleaver,
Inborn, she was caged by a witch,
Want wings to fly high and
reach ether,
Beyond sky, she wants to play,
Golden pond with pearl and
silver fish,
Such a place she wants a hut
to be build,
When she wakes up, it's realized,
It's tower too high,
She was incarcerated and not
allowed to escape,
If she gets married, a bitch with
black magic will be killed,
She will give birth to a son,
A cannon fodder and trooper,
One day when Zehava is drying
her hair long and golden,
A prince while ridding horse
get elute from his follower,
He saw golden hair and thought

it's some tree root from
heaven,
He used them and used as rope,
When he reached till window,
He fell in love with Zehava,
Asked her how she is trapped
in tower,
Zehava told him all about the
witch and push him to
go back soon,
If witch come back then she
will kill him,
Prince asked her why she is
so much worried,
Did she love him?
Zehava blush and smile,
Prince proposed her and want
to get married,
He cut down her golden hair
impend from window,
Taken her on flying carpet,
Move towards his palace,
After reaching home, they get
married,
The witch search for Zehava
for years and years,
In a forest she come across

little Brett,
Brett, son of Zehava throw an
arrow and kill the witch,
He didn't know the story of
Zehava but latter witch told him
and ask him to forgive,
She had been contorting many years from
Zehava life caged her and
reprimanded.

42. Temptation

Solicitation for his one glimpse,
No one realizes what her heart feels,
Avarice every second to let him hold her palm,
But stinginess leads it all to another
dream world,
Where rapacity teaches her level
of urge to be together,
But rule of the world teaches her to
be restraint and helm,
Being a girl, she should goad her
emotions,
Not allowed to evince her state
what all had happen,
If she manifests her desires in
front of society,
She will be considered a cocotte,
Immure and seal her lips,
Her words are not allowed to escape,
Bait is part of male world,
They can decoy play with emotions and snare...

43. Trouvaille Rondure

An Italian astronomer investigating law of motions,
Telescope to play and clear visions,
He thought all things revolve around the Earth,
He proof wrong Aristotle the great
by experimenting with balls of different sizes and weights,
he rolled them down ramps and proof that balls boasted with same acceleration independent of their mass,
Object thrown up follow parabola and teaches never trust pendulum work,
But by the time invented the first pendulum clock,
Then comes the efficient spyglass to add in the telescope,
He was the first to see craters on the moon, discovered sunspots, tracked the phases of Venus,
The rings of Saturn puzzled him, appearing as lobes and vanishing when they were edge-on,
Jupiter, Venus and Mercury then comes the Neptune,
Jupiter carries beautiful moon all around,
He supported the Copernican system,
and stated that the Earth and other planets circle the sun.
Yes...and yet it moves ... It's all his quotes...

44. Vernal Equinox

Smiling tulip bloom in mid-spring,
Rainbow colors offering sky a chiack,
Sort of saltation and earth abide,
Daffodils flowering wide paint every part of land yellow and bright,
Muscari buds blooms like cheery spikes,
A clusters of tiny grapes shade snow land with different taste,
Sweet bouquet reminds one summer days are soon to mimic,
Vault get covered by falling petals,
All creatures resile in action to fight hot weather,
Pink blooms outlined the redbug trees before leaves appear to be,
Beautiful Hyacinths brings scent as well as color,
Primrose jewels in the spring garden,
"flowering onion,"sheen is spectacular
on barren land,
Spring is often zenith and salad days for nature,
As it revives and let plants glow and sprout with alluring pleasure,
Seeds dance as burgeon state let them nourish,
They can grow well before all water get evaporated

Jasmine Panda

Miss Jasmine Panda is presently pursuing Ph.D. in Chemistry from Ravenshaw University, Odisha, India. She is a Gold Medalist and University Topper in her B.Sc. and M.Sc. She has completed an internship CSIR-SRTP in IICT Hyderabad. She holds the post of Senate Member of the University for the session 2019-20 in Academic Pursuits. She is a Governor Awardee for YRC. She has received All-Rounder Award in her 12th standard for excellence in extracurricular activities along with studies. She is a Topper throughout her career. She has been a Literary and Cultural Champion in her college days. She has also cracked a campus in Vedanta. She has hosted in numerous events including International events and has been appreciated as an anchor. She has completed Masters in Fine Arts (MFA) from Aurobindo Kala Bhawan under Bangeeya Sangeet Parishad. Apart from being a versatile orator and debater, she has been a part of 480+ anthologies till now and loves to pen down her feelings! She has compiled an anthology "Vasudhaiva Kutumbakam" under SOI publication which is also the bestseller#9. She is an amiable person interested in both Science and Literature, having a wide variety of interests like painting, sketching, acting, anchoring, debating, rangoli making, taking part in extempore, elocution, and many more... Publishing her own book someday is something which she aspires.

45. Love at first sight

At the time of divine sunset,
When our lovely eyes met!
It was as magical as "Love at first sight",
Amidst the crowd, for loneliness we fight!
Fascinated by the colours in a rainbow,
Holding each other tight for one shadow!
Just like the spectrum of love,
The purity as white as a dove!
At first sight, promising each other,
Permission granted from father and mother!
Let's be one, let's be one, just one,
Every challenge, together we can!
At the time of divine sunset,
Amidst the crowd, for loneliness we fight!
May your life be filled with garden of roses,
A lot of cheers and loads of applause!
May God bless you with all prosperity,
May our love last till eternity!
Wishing you a life full of happiness,
Wishing you a love full of craziness!
You, like a beautiful rose in my life,
It's my pleasure to get you as my wife!
I promise to be with you forever,

We both will stay happily together!
Thanks to God for gifting me,
A life with you, "you and me"!
When our lovely eyes met...
It was as magical as "Love at first sight"!
Seeking everyone's blessings this time,
Let's start our new colourful life!

46. Dream, dream and dream

Dream, dream and dream,
Dream for a big house,
Dream for a Mercedes,
Dream for a resplendent future,
Dream for an awesome life,
Dream, dream and dream,
Has no expiry date!!!
Dream, dream and dream,
Working hard to fulfill the dream,
Struggling hard to achieve it,
Managing everything to fulfill it,
Finally, never satisfied after achieving it,
Dream, dream and dream,
Has no expiry date!!!
Dream, dream and dream,
Human wants are unlimited,
Dreaming for more and more,
Fulfilling it and again dreaming for more,
Their journey never ends...
Dream, dream and dream,
Has no expiry date!!!

47. आइना

आईने में देखा जब मैंने खुद को,
एक अलग ही रूप में पाया मुझको!
क्या दिखाता है वो सिर्फ बाह्य रूप?
मुझे तो एहसास हुआ अपनी अंदरुनी स्वरूप!
बांट सकी मैं वो सारे दुख अपने,
बिना भय के बोली मेरे अनगिनत सपने!
मेरा मज़ाक उड़ाने वाला न था कोई,
स्थिर होकर सुन रहा था आइना वहीं!
कांच के टुकड़ों का है वो सम्मेलन,
सीखा मैंने करना स्वयं को नियंत्रण!
सच्चा यार मानती हूं मैं उसको,
बताती हूं उसको जो न कह पाती किसको!
दुख में संभाल लेता है मुझको ये दर्पण,
लगता है जैसे हो रहा नई ऊर्जा का आगमन!
सुनता है चुपचाप मेरी वो सारी कथा,
लगता है बांट लेता वो मेरी सारी व्यथा!
आईने के साथ ये रिश्ता कितना है अनोखा,
मेरे बुराइयों को अब नहीं कर सकती अनदेखा!
सुख में, दुख में, एकांत में, है वो मेरा सहारा,
लगता है! आज उसको कैसे नहीं निहारा!!
अंदर झांकने का यह सुनहरा अवसर,

पता नही कसिने दयिा ये सुंदर उपहार!

खुद से मलिन के लएि दरे न करो,

दौड़ के जाओ और आइने में देखो!!!

48. Never-ending Footsteps

My enthralling trip to South India!!!
Magical day and night view of Mysore Palace,
The architectural interior of Bangalore Palace!
Magical was Wonderla and Vrindavan Garden,
An evening in Ooty was no less than heaven!
Ooty's Botanical Garden, the Nature's treasure,
Visiting with family and relatives, a pleasure!
Never-ending footsteps....
My memorable trip to North India!!!
Starting our day from Mathura Vrindavan,
With a Divine experience at Akshardham!
Visiting Fatehpur Sikri and the Taj Mahal,
City Palace, Jantar Mantar, Hawa Mahal!
Visiting Red Fort, Lotus Temple and Rajghat,
An exciting tour to the famous India Gate!
Never-ending footsteps....
Never-ending footsteps....

49. The Beginning

With Love,
I believed two souls got united,
The day my life started!
In my mother's womb, my life started,
From that day, I think sadness departed!
My father took care each & every moment,
Love grew between them every second!
Smile and happiness on their way,
"Waiting to see me", they eagerly say!
I became their bond of togetherness,
Leaving all depression and stress!
The time came when I finally landed,
That was the moment most wanted!
Parents, tensed & happy, mixed feelings,
Taking energy from everybody's blessings!
The continuous cry on my little face,
Brought a smile on my parent's face!
Their love & happiness knew no bounds,
Both conversed with their eyes, no sound!
With Love,
I believed two souls got united,
The day my life started!
Forgetting all sorrows, staring at me,

An invisible contentment of feeling "we"!
Both were in pain, yet much satisfied,
For a new beginning, they were excited!
Looking around a new, different place,
After nine months of complete darkness!
Blessed to come to the planet Earth,
Yes, it's difficult to realise my worth!
I, only I, was the centre of attraction,
Receiving loads of love and affection!
Much care to nurture me the best,
Focus was on me, forgetting the rest!
Can never understand the sacrifice,
Of my parents and pay the price!
Can never feel the pain and endurance,
Throughout the journey, at a glance!
With Love,
I believed two souls got united,
The day my life started!
Taking me in their shivering hands,
A dream come true, a magic wand!
They feel heaven in their hands,
It seems, happily, their souls dance!
To the supreme, to the Almighty,
Obligations to the utmost purity!
In search of words for gratitude,
Thanksgiving was the couple's attitude!
The same excitement every year,

For my most awaited birthday, so near!
Arrangements at its peak on my B'day,
Making me feel special on this day!
Let God bless my favourite couple,
To the two souls, very beautiful!
Let God bless their one and only child,
May she can become their pride!!!
With Love,
I believed two souls got united,
The day my life started!

50. Remember!

Do you remember the Chocolates we shared together?
Remember the moments we fought together?
Remember the mischiefs we hide together?
Remember the days we spent together?
The wonderful excuses for not doing homework,
The sleepy and tired faces made in the morning!
The dreamy imaginations in the last bench,
The weird ideas for bunking classes together!
The unforgettable memories in the school bus,
The fantasies that seriously have no end!
The notorious activities in the playground,
The playful naughtiness day in and day out!
The excited we become during sports time,
The lazy n' lethargic we feel in assembly time!
The strategic plans made to obscure from father,
The unsuccessful methods to hide from mother!
Do you remember the days we spent together?
Do you really miss the days we spent together?

51. Magic of the Majesty

If I get a secret superpower,
Then first I would try to wipe out poverty,
Decreasing the hunger and it's severity!
Trying to reach out to the needy ones,
Solving their problems in a chance!!!
If I get a secret superpower,
Then, I would try to include chapters on spirituality,
In the education system, along with morality!
Highly essential, it is for today's generation,
A good human being should be one's ambition!!!
If I get a secret superpower,
Quality education to all would be my next mission,
Swiping out unemployment would be my vision!
Progress as well as prosperity in true action,
Development in all aspects of my nation!
If I get a secret superpower,
I would try to foster honesty and humanity,
Everyone would recognise their ability!
Peace and tranquility would surely prevail,
Easily everything everyone can avail!
If I get a secret superpower,
Next, I would strive for sustainable development,
Climate control would be my next achievement!

Balancing pollution levels and global warming,
Aspiring for a new start, a beautiful new morning!!!
Last but not the least, I would use my superpower,
To continuously pray to the supreme Power!
Because he is the magician of the all magic,
There lies the solution of the worldwide pandemic!!!

52. Celebration of Womanhood

Womens are beautiful angels on earth,
Everyone should understand their worth!
God-gifted cute butterflies are they,
Lights everyone's life with their ray!
Strong is their aura and personality,
No doubt of their awesome capability!
Utilising the minimum things to do a work,
Always focussed in their chosen track!
Disciplined and responsible they are,
Dedicated & committed wherever they are!
Ability to do everything inspite of obstacles,
Going through the pain of menstrual cycles!
Achieving the top target in everything,
Songs of success always they sing!
Never assume themselves the weakest,
Hard-working they are, they are the best!
Striving hard to get atleast a reward,
But nobody understands them, no award!
Moving forward to prove their notion,
Not waiting for atleast an appreciation!
Mentally and emotionally the strongest,
Be it sports or kitchen, they are the best!

Managing everything in personal life,
Outshine also in their professional life!
Love, care, affection and good deeds,
Mothers never neglect their kids!
Something beyond love, forgetting the rest,
Brother-sister bonding is the strongest!
A daughter-in-law becomes the pride,
In-laws are happy today with their chest wide!
Amidst stress & tension, providing comfort,
Husbands always look for their wife's support!
A daughter becomes the backbone of her dad,
In her presence, a family can never be sad!
Mother, sister, wife and a daughter,
In each and every role, she is a fighter!
Smoothly playing her part, she carries on,
Seeing her, everyone's depression is gone!
Still, some don't realise her importance,
Finding alone, want to take a chance!
So disgusting to hear the news every day,
Acid attacks and murders are still on the way!
Female foeticide, oh my God, so cruel!
An innocent life, how can they kill??
Domestic violence, dowry, harassment, rape!
Gender discrimination faced at every step!!!
Peace, peace & peace is everyone's silent prayer!
Let success stories of women we share!!!
The special creation of the Almighty is rare,

They are jewels, to be handled with care!
Otherwise, they can show their power,
Maa Shakti, Maa Kali with open hair!!!
Let each & every woman come forward to rule,
Let every Saraswati get educated, go to school!!!
Let every woman realise their own ability,
Let every Lakshmi be given utmost priority!
Let every woman know their inner potential,
And take steps against the anti-social!!!
Be honest, be truthful and be loyal,
The society will surely change, be social!!!
We are women, yes, we are girls,
We are our strength, we are our weakness!
Understanding true meaning of feminism,
Let's accept the culture of humanism!!!
Let's come for celebration of womanhood,
We are women, proud of ourselves, we should!!!

Ramandeep Kaur

I am Ramandeep Kaur. I am from Punjab dist Moga village Bhinder Kalan. I love writing poems, short stories and blogs.

53. जज़्बात

मैंने देखा नहीं था उसे
मैंने समझा भी नहीं था उसे
मैंने समझा तो उसके शब्द को, उसके जज़्बातो को
लखिा था उसने अपने टूटे सपनों को
उसके टूटे सपनों में मैंने देखा अपने सपने को
वो दुखी था उसने लखिा
माई खुश था मैंने पढा
उसे धोखे को शब्दो मैं लखिा
मैंने शब्दो को दलि मे लखिा
उसके धोके ने उसे कायर बना दयिा
उसके लखिे शब्दो ने मुझे शायर बना दयिा।

54. अंजान सपने

सपनों के बीच जी रही थी मैं,
असलीयत में जीती तो बकि जाती,
मैंने सपना दखेा तो था,
लकेनि कसिे बताती अपना सपना,
वो तो छनि लयिा जाता था,
सपनों को बचाने के लएि,
सपनों को जी रही थी मैं,
बनना चाहती थी आजाद़ नारी,
पर यहा जदिंगी छनि लते हैं सारी,
बकि ना जाओ, तो जीये थे सपने,
आगर नही जीती तो लटू लते अपने,
असलीयत में जनिे से अच्छा सपनों में जयिो,
सपनों में जयिोगे तो जदिंगी अबाद रहगेी।

55. माँ

माँ है वो, मेरी ही नही सबकी,
माँ तो माँ है
एक प्यारा नाम है
प्यार की कतिाब है
संस्कारों की जमात है
धूप में, छाया है
परविार का परछाया है
अंधेरे में उजाला है
प्यार का खजाना है
दुख को छुपाती है
दर्द को सह जाती है
माँ एक उजयाला है
सबकी आंख का तारा है
माँ से प्यार करो
दुनयिा अपनी अबाद करो।

56. दोस्ती

जिंदगी थी वो मेरी,
मैं उसकी थी तो वो मेरी,
वो बात थी तो भरोसा थी मैं,
वो फूल थी तो खुशबू थी मैं,

उसने सिखाया प्यार का नाम हूं मैं,
लेकिन फिर भी उसकी मुस्कान हूं,
जिंदगी यहां अंधेरों से भरी हुई थी मेरी,
उसे आकार रोशनी का दीपक जगया,
दोस्ती का नाम है जिंदगी,
या फिर ये कहं दूं की दोस्ती है तो जिंदगी है मेरी,
दोस्ती के लिए जान भी कुर्बान है,
दोस्ती पे तो इश्क भी कुर्बान है।

57. आशा

आस थी मझ्ुे,
उसक े आन े की,
या उस े मेर े जान े की,
मेरी आस म ें छ्ुपा था,
मेरा इतंजार,
लेकनि,
उसकी आस म े था उसका अंधवशि्वाश,
म ैं आस कार्त ी थी,
वो आयेगा,
लेकनि वो कहता था म ैं जाऊंगा,
ना तो वो आदमी था,
प्रभ ु भी कह नहीं सकत े,
वो सभी म े ह ै,
दखिता कसिी को,
कोन था वो सबस े पछ्ुा,
खदु उसन े बताया,
ज्यदा मत करो, क्योंकी वशि्वाश ह ूं म ैं

58. जदिंगी

मरूख है वो लोग
जो जदिंगी नहीं जीना चाहते
खदुगरज है वो लोग,
जो जदिंगी जीते तो है,
लकेनि अपने लिए नहीं,
अपने लिए,
अगर अपने लिए नहीं तो, दूसरे के लिए तो जयिो,
जदिंगी दोस्तो के लिए जआिो,
जीना है तो गैरों के लयिो जयिो,
पता नहीं कतिने रशि्ते हैं वो,
जो आपके लिए जीते हैं,
लकेनि आप उनके लिए एक जदिंगी नहीं जी सकते,
जरूरी नहीं जदिंगी गैरो के लिए जी जाए,
दोस्त,
कुछ टाइम तुम भी जदिंगी के साथ गुज़ारो,
जदिंगी तो हर वक्त साथ होती है,
बस कसिी को जदिंगी की समझ ही नहीं है,
सुख है तो कहते हैं.वाह...!
क्या जदिंगी है!! ,,
दुख है तो कहते हैं.उफ्फ्फ....!
क्या जिंदगी है?

जिंदगी दूसरो के लिए जीते जीते,
तुम्हारे लिए भी जीना चाहती है जिंदगी,
एक ही तो जिंदगी है,
ऐसे खुल कर जी लो मेरे दोस्त,
जिंदगी आप से थक जाएगी,
लेकिन आप जिंदगी से नहीं थकेंगे।

59. बंद राजकुमारी

बंद कर दयिा था उसे सबसे अच्छे टावर मे,
जा कर कह दो पजिंरे मे कैद थी वो।
नहीं देखने दयिा उसे दनुयिा को
जा कर कह दो रोशनी नहीं थी वहा
रोई भी नहीं थी वो,
लेकनि कस्मित पे हस्ती थी,
अपने शहर में रहकर भी
मयसू थी वो,
राजकुमारी थी वो महलो की,
आनंद तो वो अंधेरे का उठा रही थी,
खूबसूरत भी थी बहोत,
लेकनि,
ऐसी खूबसूरती का क्या करती?,
जसि ने उस से,
उसकी मुस्कान,उसकी आजा़दी ही छनि ली,
खोला गया एक दनि पजिंरे को, लेकनि उडाई मार चुकी थी वो,
दूर बहूत दूर,
इस कदे से,
इस दनुयिा से।

60. विश्वास

जदिंगी के रास्ते पे मैं
राही बंकर आवान्गा,
तुम्हारी ज़रूरत में
सपना बांकर आवान्गा

तुम्हारी सोच मे
जनून बांकर आवान्गा

तुम मेरे रास्ते ढूँडोगे
माई रस्तो में ग्याब हो जवांगा
तुम्हारे अपने मैं भी मैं होना
अल दिन वहा से भी उड जवागा
एह इंसान,
मैं तेरा विश्वास हुआ, तू मेरे उलट हो जाएगा।

61. भगवान हूं

अज्ज सूबा आंख खुली,
क्या दखेा,
कसिी ने नहीं दखेा,
मैंने ही दखेा,
चारो तरफ दखिाई दी रोशनी,
पता चला आज के दनि,
भगवान हूं,
सोचा बहोत कुछ करुगीं,
सब धूलो को प्रशन कृगी,
जमीर ने बोला नहीं,
आज के दनि इंसाफ करना,
कयिा भी,
कार्ति भी क्यों ना, भगवान जो थी,
भगवान दयालु होता है,
माई भी हूं,
सब धोकेबाजो को साजा दी,
गरीबो का मसीहा बनी,
भट्ट अच्छे कम कएि,
रात होई, सो गइ,
सुबह उठी तो पा चला,
दुनयिा का सबसे बड़ा क्राइम तो मैंने कयिा,

क्या किया मैंने,
घर से दूर रहकर,
माँ बाप को अनंत आश्रम छोड़ दिया।

Bikash Singh

Bikash Singh, Born and Bought up in Tinsukia, Assam, loves to write poems and stories. He also actively participates in Open Mics.

62. बेटी

नव महनिे गनि रहे थे
कसिी के इंतजार मे,
पल रही थी बेटी
मार दयिा क्यो कोख मे।
कैसी मानवता कैसा ये समाज है
सबको चाहएि माँ का पयार,
बेटी को जनम का क्यो नही अधकिार है?
उसका क्या था दोष?
जो गर्भ मे ही मार दयिा,
कैसी मजबरुी थी
जो भ्रुन हत्या का पाप कयिा?
कैसा था ये बाप,
जो एक माँ को मजबरु कयिा?
कैसा था ये बाप
जो अपने ही बेटी को मार दयिा।
कलंक है,ये दाग है
सबको अधकिार है।
जविन के बदले चल रहा मतृ्यु का ये खेल है,
कैन जमिदार है,डाकटर तो वरदान है।
इनके हाथो मे जविन के बदले मतृ्यु का भी दान है।

लालच कुछ पैसो का
करवाता इनसे गंदा काम है
धंधा इनका चलता रहता,
जेबो मे पैसा भरता रहता,
थोरी भी ना इनको शर्म है
जविन के नाम पे डाकटर ये कलंक है

63. आज के युवा

कया हो रहा है आज के युवावो को
चुन रहे है रासते वासनाएँ काम की,
जानते अंजाम काले कारनामो की
फरि भी कर रहे है पाप बनके अंजान सी।
बहक जाते है लोग छोटे-छोटे एप मे
समिट गयी है दुनयिा फोन के स्टोर मे,
मैने देखा था इसंटाग्राम रलि मे
उतार रही थी कपरे कसिी कबीर सघिं के पयार मे
इन सबको रोका बहुत था हमारी सरकार ने
उनहे भी चाहीए था पैसा बरी-बरी कार मे,
सुना था एक नाम जो बहुत बदनाम है
बेच रही थी असललि फलिमे जसिका नाम एकता कपुर है।
खोल रहा हुँ राज सुनो ये मेरी आवाज है
धयान दो ये साजसि वयापार है,
चार लोग मलिके करते ब्लैक मैलगिं से कतिनो का शकिार है
करते पैसो की मागं और ना मलिे तो उस युवा को सजाएँ मैत है।

मुझे अफसोस की ये बाजार कतिना काला है,
बरी-बरी हसतीयो ने हमारा बहुत कुछ बगिारा है,
कभी ullu कभी Alt balaji का इनहोने कयिा बहुत promotion है,
खोल कर देखो इन एप को दखिेगी असललिता ,

इनको थोरी भी ना आती शर्म है।
गंदे कर्म को धर्म बना के बेचते,
थोरी भी ना पुण्य-पाप की सोचते।
खिलौना बनाया है इनहोने महिलाओ का,
पुरुषो की थाली मे समान की तरह परोसते।
यही तो इनका असली वयापार है,
असलिलता से युवावो को मिलता पोतसाहन,
फिर पुछते महिलाएँ हवस की कयो शिकार है।
इतनी हो रही वेसयावृत की मेरी कलम रुक गयी है
मेरी सोच और कलम की ये जंग चल रही है,
कह रहा है दिल बेसुमार दर्द मै झेल गया हूँ
इसलिए इंसान की हैवानियत से डर गया हूँ।

64. दहेज प्रथा

कयो कुरूरता भरी समाज मे
कयो दहेज प्रथा को हम है मानते
नही चाहते सचचाई को हम जानना
कयो दहेज प्रथा से सदा बेटियो का करते
बोझ नही जिममेदारी है
हर किरदार निभाती है
नही होती है परेशा
बखूबी हर धर्म निभाती है
सजती है,सवरती है
सोलह सिंगार करती है
पुरुस प्रधान समाज मे
अपनी अलग पहचान बनाती है
हर कोई नही कुछ लोग ऐसे होते है
औरतो को पुतला जिसम का समझते है
घुघट मे रखते और अपनी शान बताते है
तुम इजजत घर की हो ये समझाते है
मारते-पीटते समाजकि शोषन होता है
दहेज के बदले सदा बेटियो का होता है
कई बार होता है पर बताती नही है
रक्षक ही भक्षक बन जाते है और सतायी जाती है
घर के ही कुछ लोगो की गंदी नियत होती है

घटु-घटु कर सारी जहर पी लेती है
नारी है साहब सब सह लेती है
वो शकतसिवरुपा नारी बरी अभमिानी है
आये बात सममान पे तो लर जाती है
वैसे तो शांत चेहरा हदयि शतिल होता है
जो जनम जविन को देती है
उसके साथ अनयाय कयो
दहेज के बदले सैदा बेटयिो का कयो
कुछ मजगुरयिो के खातरि इनहे दलदल मे धकेला जाता है
वयापार जसिम का करवाया जाता है
कछ नामद्र,कुछ पैसो के खातरि अंजाम ऐसो कामो को देते है
नोचते खरोचते गहरा घाव बना देते है
कुछ जररुतो के खातरि बयापार जसिम का करवाया जाता है
जहा भी जाऊँ शोषन महलिावो का होते देखा है
यहा भी सैदा बेटयिो का होते देखा है|

65. सजा

कसिी ने कहा तु कसिी और की महोबबत हो गयी है
सजा ये कैसी मलि रही है
ये इशक इबादत तेरे बस मे नही
हर रसमो-रविाज सजा हो रही है
जाने ये कैसी सजा मलि रही है
महोबबत मेरे हसिसे की औरो मे बट रही है
तुमहारी खुशी उसके गले लपिट रही है
जाने ये कैसी सजा मलि रही है
तुमहारा सर उसके कंधे पर
वो जुलफो की छाँव मे रहता है
घनी दुपहरी मे महोबबत की छाँव लेता है
हमारे हसिसे की छाँव औरो मे बट रही है
जाने ये कैसी सजा मलि रही है
महोबबत है रहमत इसे सजा मत कहो
नफरत है महोबबत मत कहो
आज मेरे साथ,कल उसके साथ
इसे औरत मत कहो
दखिावटी दुपटटे को शर्म-हया मत कहो
नफरत है वकिास महोबबत मत कहो

66. बचपन

वो बचपन वाला पयार कहा
सपना आँखो मे कहा
पापा वाला कधां कहा
माँ वाली रोटी कहा
बचपन वाला पयार कहा
अब नदिं की जगह आँखो मे आँसू है
खुश थे बचपन था,अब परेशानी है
पयार पापा का अब नही मलिता
कतिना मजगुर हो गया,जमाने से लड़ने को
कलेजा मोम था,पतथर बना लयिा
बोझ सहते-सहते जमिमेदारयिो का,बचपन छनि गया
देख लो पापा मै बरा हो गया
नालायक समझ रहे थे,लायक नकिल गया
बदमाशि बचपन मे थी
अब काम होता है,सफिट डबल होता है
चंद पैसो के लएि डाट पर जाते है
देख लो पापा मै बरा हो गया
देखो माँ जवानी अब बचपन खोज रहा
तुमहारी हाथो कि रोटी खोज रहा
उँगली पकर कर साथ चलने को पापा का हाथ खोज रहा
ना जाने छोटे से बरा कब हो गया

देख लो पापा मेरा बचपन छिन गया
घर का हर एक खलिैना
खेला जसिसे मै करता था
जसिमे मेरी यादे थी
हँसी और हाहाकारे थे
अब वो खलिौना कबार मे बकि रहा
रोक लो पापा,मेरा बचपन छिन रहा
रोक लो माँ,मेरा बचपन छिन रहा

67. बिछिर गये

चाहतो की भड़ि मे अजनवी हम हो गये
ना तुम रूके,ना हम रूके
ये भड़ि थी क बिछिर गये
हौसला था मगर,चाहतो की भड़ि मे
हम मलिंगे सड़क के कसिी मोर पे
ना हम रूके,ना तुम रूके
ये भड़ि थी क बिछिर गये
ये इशक था बेफजिुल,चाहतो मे कयो घरि गये
ये दलि धरक रहा,कयो धरकनो से डर गये
ना तुम रही,ना मै रहा
ना दलि रहा,ना धरक रहा
दर बदर भटकता रहा मै उसकी तलाश की में
ढुढता रहा उसे उसी चाय की दुकान पे
ना वो आयी,ना उसे हम मलिे
ये भड़ि थी क बिछिर गये
हमे अंदाजा था भला,बछिरना है एक दनि
चाहतो की भड़ि मे बछिरने से कयो डर गये
ना तुम रहे,ना हम रहे
ये भड़ि थी क बिछिर गये

68. कहानी

हजारो चेहरे है
हजारो है कहानयिाँ
राज कतिनी गहरी है
गहरी है कहानयिा
कहानयिो का कया
हर रोज नही कहानी है
हर रोज नये चेहरे है
कौन कसिका हुआ है जो अब होगा
खुन तो एक ही है
फरि भाई-भाई दुशमन कयो है
माँ-बाप तो अपने है
फरि वृद्ध आक्षम कयो है
कभी माँ उँगली पकरा कर गावँ घुमाती थी
ये बुढ़ापा कैसा है
आज गोद मे लिए माँ को असपताल घुमता हुँ
मुझे समझ नही आता ए खुदा
ये कानुन तेरा कैसा है
जो कल था वो आज नही
जो आज है वो कभी नही
मै आशा और नराशा के जंजरिो मे फँसा हुआ
यँहा पग-पग पर जंजरि है,मै जंजरिो मे बंधा हुआ

ए खुदा इंसाफ कर दरे से कर भले कर
सहमे हुए को हमिमत दे,भटके हुए को रासता दखिा
माँ मेरी रोती है दखुो को समटे कर
मै रठु जाउ तो मनातहिै
ना मानं ु तो रोकर मनातहिै
ए खुदा,ये दु:खो का बादल कतिना काला है
मेरी माँ को हर बार रुलातहिै

Rohit Gupta

Rohit Gupta is from Doomdooma, Tinsukia, Assam. He is a Science Teacher by profession but also follows his passion for writing.

69. पहली बार खुद को नरिाश कयिा

दलि दहल उठा, शरीर सहम उठा।
वो दनि, जब मैंने खुद को नरिाश कयिा।
दनि् था २१, सन् था १६, माह था भई का,
उस दनि क्यों ना रहे 'याद,
था वह बरहवीं का परणिाम का दनि
परीक्षा फल घोषति हुआ उत्तीर्ण भी हुआ।
पर जैसा चाहा, वैसा ना हुआ।
प्रथम श्रेणी भी आ गई,
पर मन चाहा अंक न आया,
उस दनि पहली बार मैं खुद को नरिाश पाया।
वो दनि हमेशा याद आएगी, जब
जब देगी बरहवीं का परणिाम
क्योंकि उस दनि, मैं पाया था खुद को नरिाश|

70. मुखौटे के पीछे

दर्द छुपाना आँसु छुपाना लोगों के प्रती प्यार को न जता पाना।
कहते हैं, मतलबी का यार हूँ मैं, समय पर काम न आता हूँ,
कैसे बताऊ मेरे अंदर की आत्म का दर्द जो मैं मुखौटे के पीछे छुपा रखा हूँ।
त्वचा पर लगी आग को,
मैं छीपा कर रखा चेहरे की शांति को दबा कर रखा हूँ।
अकेलापन मुझे न खा जाएं इसलिए दोस्त बनाए रखा ई

71. एक बहुत बूढ़ा व्यक्ति

रहा मे चलते मिला एक व्यक्ति से,
वृद्ध थे काफी, बाबा से दिखते थे।
फटे कपड़े, झुली दाढी,
ठिठुरती हड्डी दर्शाती थी,
उनको जीवन की अंतिम रूपी कहाना|
मुझरा रहा ना गया, मैंने पूछ दिया।
ए! बाबा, इस वृद्ध उमर में,
आपने किस यात्रा पर चल दिये
उनकी जवाब सुन टपक परे आँसू नयन से
बोले धन की लोभ में बेटा खोया
बेटा ढूंढने निकला तो, खोया मैंने धन ।
न बेटा मिला, न धन,
अंत में औरत ने भी छोरा संगा मैंने उन्हें हृदय से लगाया,
बोला चल बाबा मेरे संग,
मेरा नहीं कोई इस संसार में,
तुझे पाकर पाया सारा धन|

72. अवकाश स्मृति

अवकाश वे लम्हे हैं जब हम खुल कर मज़े करते हैं
याद सज़ाकर, संग्रहित कर रखते हैं
ऐसे ही कुछ अवकाश की स्मृति बनाए रखे हैं
की,गए थे घुमने, नई जगह पर नई मित्र बनारे रखे हैं
रहन-सहन, भेष-भाषा अलग हुआ,
खान-पान का अलग आया स्वाद
वो यात्रा ओर कोई नहीं,
थी मणिपुर की राजधानी इंफाल।
भूला नहीं अब भी उसे,
बीते जिसके हुए पाँच झाल यादो की छवी बना,
रह गई स्मृति जीवन साथ|

73. ईश्वर पूरी कर दे मुराद मेरी

वर्षों बीत गई, विवाह के बन्धन बांधे,
अब आई वरिाण जिन्दगी में बहार है।
वर्षों की मुराद पूरी हुई,
जुड़ने को नया परिवार है।
खुशी की किलकारी गूंज रही हैं,
पर मन की चाह दबाए नहीं जा रहा है।
हर्षोल्लास का माहोल घर में सभी लोग मनाए हैं।
लोग, जो बोलते थे,
तुच्छ शब्द हम पर,
आज गुणगाण गए हैं।
वर्षों बाद फिर जीवन में खुशी के पल ए आए हैं।

Printed by Libri Plureos GmbH in Hamburg,
Germany